SOCCER
SHOWDOWNS

Rob Childs

Illustrated by Stephen Player

OXFORD

1
Shooting practice

'Shoot!'

The boy did as he was told, but scooped his shot high over the crossbar.

'Don't panic,' cried the teacher, Mr Smith, 'keep it down.'

Mr Smith rolled a ball towards the next player in the practice group. It happened to be the school team's leading scorer, Michael Medway.

'Take on the defender, Michael. Let's see you get past him before shooting.'

That was easier said than done.

The defender blocking his path to goal was Josh Parker, the hard-tackling captain.

'C'mon, then, Mike,' Josh called out with a laugh, 'bet you can't score.'

'How are you going to stop me?'

'No trouble. I'll trip you up if I have to!'

Michael tried to beat Josh for speed, but his friend was just as quick. Michael was forced wide, away from the goal, and he had to shield the ball with his body.

Josh was breathing hard down his neck. 'Give in?'

Michael replied with action, not words. His sharp twist and turn caught the captain by surprise. A shooting chance suddenly opened up and he took it. Josh's crunching tackle was a fraction too late. As the boys tumbled to the ground, Michael saw the ball skim past the goalkeeper's dive – but also just past the far post.

'I won,' Josh claimed as they pulled one another up. 'I knocked you off-balance.'

'Rubbish! I'd already shot.'

'You still missed.'

Mr Smith approached them. 'No time for chat, you two. Get ready, Josh, next man's coming in.'

That wasn't quite true. The player running at goal was in fact a girl, Charlotte, better known as Charlie.

'Show Mike how it's done, Charlie,' cried a team-mate.

Josh was struggling to get back into position in time to make a challenge.

Charlie worked the ball on to her stronger left foot and let fly before Josh reached her.

The keeper got his hand to the ball, but it brushed past his fingers and flashed high into the net.

'Great goal!' said Michael. 'We'll have another one of those tomorrow.'

She smiled. 'Hope so. I've not scored in the cup yet.'

'Best place to do it is in the final.'

The footballers of Colford Primary School had been looking forward to playing in the cup final for weeks. They won their semi-final game well before Easter and had almost wished the holidays away. They could hardly wait to return to school for the big match!

It was Baz's go now to try his luck against the Colford captain. Baz was Michael's main partner in attack. His dribbling skills could turn people inside-out when he was on form. If he wasn't on form, he dribbled himself dizzy in circles.

Josh was on his toes, alert, determined that Baz was not going to make a fool out of him.

As Baz trotted forwards, Josh backed off, waiting for the right moment to strike. He fixed his eyes on the ball so as not to be put off by Baz's fancy footwork.

Baz jinked this way and that, but he tried one side-step too many.

He lost control of the ball for just a split-second and Josh pounced. Josh put his full weight into the tackle and Baz was left sitting on his bottom in the penalty area.

'I know all your little tricks, Baz,' Josh laughed, booting the ball away.

8

'I've watched you do them all season.'

Josh and Baz were team-mates, not just for the school, but also for their Sunday League side, Red Star Dynamos. Baz gave a shrug, then jumped up and wandered back to join the group of players. He didn't mind them giggling at him. 'Don't reckon I'm going to get any sleep tonight,' he admitted, 'I'm feeling dead nervous.'

Michael grinned. 'You'll be OK in the morning as soon as we kick off. I dreamed we both scored a hat-trick!'

He and Baz made a good pair up front. Michael was tall and strong. Baz was small and fast. The two strikers had helped each other score many goals for the school.

They knew that they faced their most difficult test of the season in the final. They were up against the school with the best defence.

Lynton Juniors had won the league title easily, letting in only six goals in fourteen matches.

'Right, get into teams of four now for a quick game,' Mr Smith called out, and then he picked on the goalkeeper. 'C'mon, Will, you're getting fat and slow. Stop messing around with those gloves. You don't need them for this.'

Will grinned confidently. He and the footballers were used to the way old Smithy liked to grumble. It was taken as a sign of respect to be insulted by him. The teacher seemed to enjoy moaning at the better players even more than he did at the others. Praise was rare indeed.

Will soon showed how good a goalkeeper he was. Baz tested him with a shot that dipped late, but Will had his body behind the ball and blocked it. The rebound ran loose to Charlie, who tried to flick it back over his head as he lay on the ground.

Will's reflexes were laser sharp. He sprang to his feet again and grabbed the ball with both hands.

'I said you were getting too slow,' Mr Smith reminded him. 'You should have held on to that first shot.'

Will threw the ball out to Michael on the wing. The striker neatly dummied his way past one opponent and then Josh stepped in to whisk the ball off his toes.

Michael and Josh were usually on opposite sides. They were good mates, but they liked playing against each other. There was more fun in winning that way.

They were going to be on opposite sides on Sunday too. The coming weekend was a feast of football for many of the Colford players.

After Saturday's Cup Final, Red Star Dynamos faced a showdown with Forest Rangers to decide which team finished top of their Sunday League division. Josh was captain of the Dynamos and Michael captained the Rangers.

'Hope I'm marking you on Sunday,' Josh said. 'That'd give me an easy afternoon.'

'Don't count on it. I might play in defence myself.'

'Chicken! Just 'cos you know you won't get a kick in attack.'

Michael laughed. 'Knowing you, I'd get lots of kicks – most of them on my legs!'

'Hey! Cut that out!' barked Mr Smith. 'I hope you two aren't talking about Sunday. You know I've banned that. I want your full attention on tomorrow's match.'

Josh put on his innocent look. 'Sunday? What's happening then, Mike, do you know?'

'Search me,' Mike said, with a smile and a shrug.

'Good job too,' said the teacher, slipping them both a sly wink. 'First things first, right?'

They all agreed on that. The school always came first on Saturdays.

'Right, let's play on!'

2

Heads!

SPLAAATTT! The football smacked against the outside wall of the changing room and left a round, wet stain on the brickwork.

'Hey! Watch it!'

'Sorry, Mike,' chuckled Baz, 'I sliced that one a bit.'

Michael Medway was not amused. His soccer shirt was sprayed with drops of dirty water.

'Huh! I just hope your shooting is better than that in the match. You nearly knocked my head off.'

Baz laughed. 'Old Smithy often says we run about like headless chickens. At least you wouldn't be able to hear him shouting at us any more.'

Michael finished tying his boot laces and stood up. 'Maybe not, but I wouldn't be able to score any more headers either. I get half my goals with my head.'

'Do you think we can beat Lynton today?' said Baz.

'I don't see why not. We drew against them in the League.'

'Yeah, but that was before Christmas. They've won their last six games, so Pele says.'

Pele played with Baz for the Dynamos and he was also Lynton Juniors' top striker. Michael knew all about Pele, nicknamed after the world famous Brazilian soccer star. His speed and skills were a real danger. They were going to be seeing a lot of one another this weekend.

'It's about time Lynton lost, then, I reckon,' said Michael. 'C'mon, I'm ready. Let's go and warm up.'

He ran over to the ball and flicked it up into the air. As it came down, he juggled it on his knee a couple of times and then hit it on the volley to Baz – right to his feet.

'Show off!' laughed his striking partner. 'Bet Lynton won't let you do any circus tricks like that this morning. You know who will be marking you – Chopper!'

Michael shrugged. 'Or you.'

'Not me. He lets somebody else take care of little kids like me. Pele says that Chopper likes to cut big 'uns like you down to size.'

'Pele's been having a lot to say for himself, by the sound of it,' Michael said with a smile.

He was trying to make light of meeting Chopper again, but the Lynton captain was not somebody Michael wanted to play against every week.

The tough tackling centre-back made Josh seem like a softie. Michael still had the scar on his knee from when Rangers played Chopper's Tigers side on a cold, frosty Sunday back in January.

When Michael and Baz joined their team-mates on the pitch, they were given an equally frosty greeting by Mr Smith.

'About time too,' he growled, 'I was beginning to think you two must have gone home.'

'One of Mike's laces broke,' said Baz. 'I was just waiting for him.'

'That's all we need in the final. A player whose boot keeps flying off all the time!'

'It's OK, Mr Smith,' said Michael, 'I've got it sorted out now.'

'You'd better have, lad, and I hope they're your best shooting boots as well. We need a goal or two from you.'

The Lynton team were even later turning up on the pitch. Their teacher had kept them in the changing room for as long as possible. He was busy talking about positions and tactics, but all the boys wanted to do was go out and play football.

'Give it everything you've got – one hundred per cent effort,' he demanded. 'Win this match and you've done the League and Cup Double!'

'Here they come,' cried Baz as the white shirts at last made their appearance. 'Chopper's leading them out. He sure looks in a mean mood.'

'C'mon, the Juniors!' shouted one of their supporters, 'you can beat this lot from Colford.'

The Lynton players realized that victory was not going to be as easy as that. They were expecting a tough battle. Several of them, like Pele, played with members of the Colford side on Sundays and knew how keen they were to win too.

'Feels a bit strange, doesn't it?' said Baz as he and Michael took shots at Will in goal. 'I mean, today I'm hoping that Will keeps a clean sheet, but tomorrow I want to score six against him myself.'

'No way!' laughed Michael. 'He'd never live it down if he let you do that. Besides, I'll make sure you don't even get a shot in.'

'Are you definitely going to play in defence?'

Michael nodded. 'Sweeper. That's my favourite position really, but old Smithy always puts me up in attack with you for the school.'

'That's because we're such a deadly partnership,' Baz grinned. 'He doesn't want to break it up.'

Josh Parker jogged up to the centre-circle for the toss. He shook hands with the referee and then with Lynton's captain, but it wasn't in friendship.

'We're going to thrash you, Parker.'

'No way, Chopper,' Josh replied, grimly, 'the Cup's ours.'

'OK, lads, cut it out,' the referee told them. 'That's not a very good way to start. It's how you play the game that's important, not who wins it.'

Chopper stared at the referee. 'This is a Cup Final,' he stated, flatly, 'of course we want to win it.'

The referee sighed. 'Just play to the whistle and don't talk back. No arguing – understand, both of you?'

The captains nodded, not really listening to what he was saying. They were too busy glaring at each other.

'Heads!' called Josh as the referee flipped the coin. A few moments later the Queen's head glinted in the morning sunshine on the bare earth of the centre-spot.

'We'll stay as we are,' he said, pleased with his little triumph over Chopper. 'You can have kick-off.'

'Concentrate,' yelled Mr Smith from the touchline, 'we don't want to give away any daft goals through sloppiness. Get those gloves on, Will. The grass is still wet.'

The goalkeeper was already pulling them on. Michael's last shot had just slipped through his fingers. Will didn't want to make any mistakes like that in the actual match, not in front of so many people. The Cup Final had attracted quite a big crowd.

Nobody, however, expected such a dramatic start to the game. Will was the first Colford player to touch the ball, and that was to do the job he hated most – picking the ball out of the back of his own net.

'I don't believe it!' groaned Mr Smith.

3

First half

'GOOAALL!' screamed Pele, 'GOOAALL!'

Pele always went mad after scoring a goal. He raced towards the corner flag, doing a clumsy forward roll along the way. Pele would have loved to do a somersault or handspring, but he was better at football than gymnastics.

It had taken Lynton Juniors only three passes from the kick-off to send Pele clear down the left wing. The Colford defence was caught stone cold.

Even Josh was in no position to stop him.

'Block the shot!' he cried, as Pele cut inside into the penalty area.

It was too late. The shot was already speeding towards its target. Will had started to come off his line to narrow the shooting angle, but he was well-beaten by the early strike. The goalkeeper made a desperate effort to reach the ball, but it flew beyond his dive into the net.

Pele flashed his Dynamos captain a cheeky grin as he trotted back to the halfway line. 'Told you I'd score against you in the Cup Final. Easy!'

Josh sighed and glanced at Baz. 'We'll never hear the last of that now. He'll be rubbing it in for ages.'

'Not if we win,' said Baz. 'That will be the only way to hit back and shut him up.'

Josh clapped his hands to encourage his team. 'C'mon, forget about that. Nothing we can do about it now. Just get on with the game.'

Mr Smith's shouts were not helping.

'Hopeless! I warned you. You just let that winger walk straight through you.'

'Huh! Pele was hardly walking,' Baz grunted. 'Bet he's the quickest player on the pitch.'

The first goal-scoring chance for Colford fell to Charlie, the only girl in the match. She swapped passes with a team-mate to make progress up the left-wing, then she switched the ball across to Baz on the right.

Charlie ran on in the hope of a return pass, but Baz curled the ball high into the goal-mouth. Michael and Chopper jumped for it together and it was the huge defender who won their heading duel.

The ball didn't travel very far. It dropped at Charlie's feet on the edge of the penalty area and she struck it on the half-volley. The snapshot was goal-bound but the Lynton keeper, Liam, made a smart save on the line.

'That's more like it,' cried a Colford supporter. 'Keep it up!'

It did mark the start of a good spell for Colford. They put together a string of dangerous attacks, but each one seemed to be ended by Chopper's head or his size seven boots.

'Easy to see why they don't let many goals in,' muttered Mr Smith to one of the Colford parents. 'That captain of theirs is built like a battleship.'

No sooner were those words out of his mouth when Chopper made his first mistake of the game. He slipped and failed to cut out a pass that he would normally swallow up. Michael was so surprised to find himself in the clear that he hesitated for a moment.

'Go for goal!' Baz screamed. 'Go, go, go!'

Michael went. With only the goalkeeper to beat, an equalizer looked almost certain. Michael expected to score at least seven times out of ten in that kind of situation. Sadly, this was one of the other three.

Liam rushed out to meet him and dived to his left to make a fine stop.

But it was Michael's right boot that he caught. The ball had ballooned over the crossbar.

Everyone laughed when they realized what had happened; well, nearly everyone. Mr Smith was the odd one out.

'Um ... I think this might be yours,' sniggered Liam as he handed over the boot. 'Any idea where it came from?'

Michael glanced down at his foot and shook his head. 'No – complete mystery to me!'

Chopper butted in, 'Ah, poor little boy. Didn't Mummy teach you how to tie your laces!'

It was Michael's dad who came to his rescue. As the striker hobbled across to the touchline for repairs, Mr Medway tore out the lace from his own walking boot to replace the broken one.

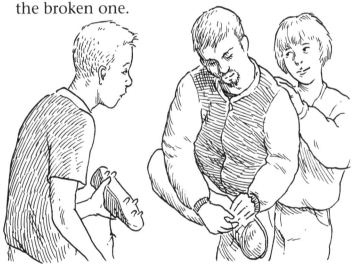

While Michael was off the field, Lynton went close to increasing their lead. Pele dummied past his marker and hit a low cross that the centre-forward, Hanif, met at the near post.

Hanif's clever touch would have beaten most goalkeepers, but not his Rangers' teammate. Will was perfectly placed to turn the ball past the upright for a corner.

Will pulled the number nine to his feet. 'Close, Hanif,' he smiled. 'Sorry, I just couldn't let you score.'

'Plenty of time yet. I'll put one past you later. That's a promise.'

'Don't make promises you can't keep.'

'I always keep my promises,' Hanif said, grinning. 'You know that, Will.'

The referee waved Michael back on in time to help Colford defend the corner. The ball sailed over to the far post where Chopper rose above Michael to head powerfully towards the goal. Will could only watch, open-mouthed, but the ball clipped the top of the crossbar and passed out of play.

'C'mon, Mike,' Josh moaned, 'he's out-jumping you every time.'

'You mark him, if you think you can do better,' Michael snapped back. 'He's all elbows.'

The captain scowled and changed the subject. 'Is your boot going to stay on now?'

'Hope so. I've got it tied up really tight.'

'Well, get up the other end and score us a goal. Make up for that one you messed up.'

With five minutes to go before the interval, Lynton was still 1-0 ahead.

Then Dinesh, Colford's left-midfield player, set up a chance for the equalizer. He'd been having a quiet game up to that point, but now he swept over a centre into the danger area around the penalty spot, and Michael threw himself head-first at the ball.

A fraction of a second later and Michael might have lost his front teeth. Chopper lunged at the ball wildly with his boot, only just missing his opponent's face. But Michael's bravery was rewarded. The ball glanced off his forehead and left Liam wrong-footed.

The goalkeeper could only flap a hand at the ball, as if waving it goodbye as it passed him into the corner of the net.

'Great goal, Mike!' Baz screamed into his ear as he lay flat out in the goal-mouth.

Michael didn't have a chance to reply. He was soon buried under a pile of team-mates.

Michael's equalizer gave his team a great boost of confidence.

Two minutes later, it was Dinesh's turn to receive the hero treatment. Charlie laid the ball back into his path and he steered it calmly past the helpless Liam.

As the Colford players mobbed Dinesh in celebration, Liam lashed out at his defenders.

'Where's the marking?' he demanded, angrily. 'Who was picking up that kid? Get it sorted out, Chopper.'

It wasn't perhaps a wise thing to do. Chopper thought that Liam was blaming him for the goal and he lost his temper. Just when it looked like a fight might start up, Josh stepped between them to protect his Dynamos goalkeeper.

'Break it up, guys,' he cried.

'You keep out of it,' stormed Chopper. 'This has nothing to do with you.'

'Yes, it has. Liam's playing in goal for us tomorrow and I want him in one piece, OK?'

There was no doubt which team enjoyed half-time more. Colford was now 2-1 up. The happy Colford camp could hear raised voices coming from the Lynton group thirty metres away.

'I don't suppose they're used to letting two goals in like that so close together,' said Josh. 'I can't even remember when Liam was last beaten twice on a Sunday.'

'He'll have to get used to it,' Michael smirked. 'It could be habit forming.'

'How do you mean?'

'Because it's going to happen to him again tomorrow!'

4
Magic!

'Foul, Ref!'

The referee agreed with the winger's loud appeal and blew his whistle. 'Direct free-kick.'

Pele jumped to his feet and got ready to take the kick himself. It was well outside the penalty area but he still wanted a shot at the goal.

Pele was feeling frustrated. He hadn't seen much of the ball in the second half. Mr Smith told Dinesh at half-time to help the full-back to mark him, and together they had given Pele very little space. Now Dinesh had mistimed his tackle and tripped up the winger.

'Form a wall,' cried Josh. 'Pele's wicked from there.'

The captain knew how well Pele could strike a dead-ball. He had scored a number of goals for the Dynamos from free-kicks like this.

Pele lashed the ball towards the goal and Baz was the unlucky one that took the full force of the blast. The ball hit him in the stomach and he dropped with a grunt as all the air was knocked out of him.

Baz lost interest in the action after that.

He was too busy trying to breathe again.

The ball had rebounded to Pele and he chipped it over into the goal-mouth. Chopper, Josh and Will all went for it at the same time and they collided with a crunch in mid-air. The keeper just managed to punch the ball off Chopper's head, but he felt as if he'd been hit by a ground-to-air missile.

The referee blew for another free-kick, but this one was in Colford's favour.

'Dangerous challenge,' he said, looking at Chopper. 'You went more for the goalie than the ball. Calm down.'

'What about him?' fumed Chopper, pointing at Josh. 'He fouled me too. Should be a penalty for us.'

'Don't argue with me, lad, I warned you before. Free-kick for Colford!'

The game didn't restart until both Baz and Will had fully recovered.

'That's the last time I stand in the wall when Pele's around,' Baz wheezed. 'I was nearly sick.'

'Worth it,' Josh said with a grin. 'You stopped him scoring, that's the main thing.'

Colford weathered the storm and for a time Liam was the busier of the two goalkeepers. Michael, Baz and Charlie all tested him out with good shots, and Baz struck the post with one that skidded past Liam's dive.

It came as a shock to Colford, therefore, when Lynton broke away to equalize.

The goal was a bad one to give away. Colford had been pressing forward in search of another goal themselves when Liam's long kick soared over the halfway line. Dinesh had strayed too far upfield and it was a race between the full-back and Pele for the ball.

There could only be one winner. Pele sprinted clear and tried to push the ball wide of the oncoming keeper. Will stuck out a foot at the last moment and blocked the shot. Colford's relief was short-lived. Hanif was following up and slid the rebound coolly into the unguarded net.

The scorer smiled at his Rangers team-mate. 'Told you I always keep my promises, Will.'

Mr Smith, however, was furious. 'Serves you right,' he yelled. 'That will teach you a lesson. You were already dreaming about your winners' medals.'

'He's off again,' muttered Baz.

'He could be worse, I guess,' said Michael. 'At least old Smithy isn't as bad as some of the parents you hear on Sundays. Y'know, all the swearing and that on the touchline.'

'He probably does that under his breath!'

A few minutes later, the ball was in the back of Colford's net once more. Will had not even made much of an effort to stop it.

'Wake up, boy!' Mr Smith cried out in horror. 'You just stood and watched it go in.'

Only then did the teacher realize that the whistle had already gone for offside. He shuffled his feet sheepishly.

There were no more scares after that. When the referee blew for full-time, the teams were still level at 2-2.

'Five minutes each way extra time now,' he told them.

'What if it's still a draw then?' asked Baz. 'Is there a replay?'

'No – it'll be decided on penalties!'

Mr Smith quickly gathered the players around him. 'You should have won this already,' he grumbled. 'Now you've got to go out and win it again.'

'Who's going to take the penalties?' asked Dinesh.

'Why, are you volunteering?' grinned Josh.

'No way. I don't want to miss one.'

The teacher sighed. 'I can see we might be here all day at this rate – and I haven't done my shopping yet.'

'C'mon, team,' Josh urged as they lined up again for the start of the extra period, 'you heard what the man said. Let's get this game won and send old Smithy off shopping.'

There was no score in the first half. The nearest either team came to a goal was when Michael's long-range drive swerved the wrong side of the post.

The longer the game went on, the more tired the players became. As a result, the marking was not so tight, and both teams missed good chances to win the game. Then it looked as if Lynton had finally clinched it.

Will's weak goal-kick went straight to an unmarked opponent who slipped the ball through to Pele. The winger did the rest.

He was dancing off towards the corner flag to start the victory party even before the ball slapped into the net.

Lynton paid the full price for celebrating too early. The game was not over yet. In a last desperate attack, Michael linked up with Baz outside the area and then flicked the ball on to Charlie.

Her shot was low and true. She aimed it deliberately for the far corner and the ball snaked wide of Liam and just inside the post. It was unstoppable.

'What a goal!' cried Michael. 'You're a hero, Charlie.'

'Um … I think that should be heroine,' grinned Baz.

'You're right about one thing, Mike,' she laughed, 'there is no better place to score your first cup goal than in the Final. It's a magic feeling.'

All the players were grateful to hear the final whistle. They had given everything, but nobody was able to relax. They still had to face the nerve-racking drama of the penalty shoot-out …

5

Shoot-out

'Right, we'll have you, you and you.'

Each team needed three penalty-takers for the shoot-out and Mr Smith picked his trio without any fuss. He didn't even ask Baz, Michael and Josh if they wanted to do it.

'Nobody's going to blame you if you miss,' he told them. 'Just get it on target. Force the keeper to make a save.'

'Huh! It's OK for him to say that,' muttered Baz, whose turn was first. 'He won't have to put up with Liam afterwards.'

'I'll go last,' insisted Josh. 'That's the captain's job if everything depends on the final penalty.'

Baz gave a snort. 'Yeah, it also means you might not have to take one at all. We could have won it 2-0 by then – or lost it.'

Michael felt a little more confident than the others. He was used to taking penalties for the school and for Rangers. 'Does Liam know which side you two like to hit them?' he asked. 'I mean, you train with him every week.'

'I haven't got a favourite side,' Josh admitted. 'Pele's the Dynamos' spot-kick king. We always leave it to him.'

'He's bound to take one of Lynton's,' added Baz. 'I wonder who else it will be?'

They were soon to find out.

Josh won the toss again. 'We'll have first shot,' he told Chopper. 'Put the pressure on you lot.'

'Not if you miss, you won't.'

'Are you taking one of them?' asked Josh.

'Nah, I'm letting the others get on with it,' answered Chopper.

'What's up? Haven't you got the bottle?'

Chopper glared at him. 'You're going to wish you hadn't said that. I've got more bottle than a drinks factory!'

Baz strolled towards the penalty spot, trying to look a lot more cool and casual than he felt. The butterflies were churning inside him.

Liam was leaning against the post, smirking at him. 'No way you'll get this past me, Baz, no way!'

Baz didn't bother to reply. He was happy to let his boot do the talking.

As he placed the ball carefully on the white penalty spot, he decided to put his kick to Liam's left. He took several steps backwards and waited for the whistle.

'Stay on your line, keeper, until the ball is kicked,' said the referee as Liam strayed forward to delay the penalty a few seconds. The goalkeeper wanted to add to any nerves that Baz might have.

The whistle blew and Baz ran in. In the last stride, Liam moved to his left and caused Baz to have a sudden change of mind. He side-footed the ball the other way and the late switch proved fatal.

Baz struck the ball cleanly, but not hard enough, or wide enough. Liam barely had to dive. He simply fell on top of the ball and parried it away to safety.

A great roar went up from the Lynton supporters. A low groan escaped from the throats of Colford's. Baz was rooted to the spot. He wished the ground would open up and swallow him out of sight.

'Sorry, pal,' said Liam, 'had to do it.'

Baz nodded dumbly, turned and trudged back, head down, to where the others were waiting in the centre-circle. Charlie was the first to try and console him.

'Just one of those things,' she said. 'You did your best.'

He shook his head. 'If that was my best, I hate to think what my worst would be like.'

'Forget it, Baz,' said Dinesh, 'we've still got Mike and Josh to put things right for us.'

'And we've still got Will,' added Charlie, crossing her fingers as she spoke. 'He'll take some beating.'

At that moment, Will was staring at Lynton's first kicker in amazement – it was Liam.

'Is this allowed, Ref?' Will asked.

'Anybody in the team can take a penalty; even the goalkeeper, if he wants to.'

It was a surprise move by Lynton, but Liam was a good all-round footballer. He had scored two goals for the school when playing in midfield.

Liam drove the ball hard and straight – dead straight. Will hadn't dived. He stood his ground and the ball smacked him in the chest. It hurt, but not half as much as it would have done to let Liam score past him.

Liam shook his head in disbelief and trooped into goal again for his own turn between the posts. 'Perhaps I should stick to saving penalties,' he muttered to himself.

He didn't even manage to do that now. Michael stroked his penalty high to the right, beating Liam all ends up. Michael punched the air in delight.

'1-0 to Colford,' announced the referee.

Hanif was just as accurate. His penalty was swept to Will's left, into the bottom corner. Again, the goalkeeper hadn't dived, but this time his gamble failed to pay off.

'Scores level at 1-1,' the referee called out. 'Last go coming up for each team.'

The tension mounted on the final kickers, Josh and Pele. They were good friends, but each one was now hoping that the other was going to miss. Charlie couldn't bear to watch as Josh strode forward. She turned her back and stared at the school building instead.

As Josh placed the ball, Liam began to sway on the line, hoping to distract his Dynamos captain. Josh didn't even glance his way.

'Here goes,' Josh murmured, 'hit and hope.'

Josh knew he couldn't slot the ball exactly where he wanted it to go. He was going to rely on sheer power.

On the signal, he ran in and blasted the ball as hard as he could. For a heart-stopping moment, he thought it was going over the bar. Then it clipped the underside of the woodwork and billowed out the netting. Liam had no chance.

'Glad I wasn't in the way of that rocket,' Liam grunted. 'Might have knocked me into the net with it.'

Josh slapped Will on the back. 'We're 2-1 up. Save this one and we've won the Cup!'

The goalkeeper gave his captain a lopsided grin.

'Yeah, thanks, that's all I needed to know. And what if I don't?'

'Then it's sudden-death. We carry on doing this till one team scores and the other misses.'

'Sounds like old Smithy's never going to get his shopping done!'

The cheers and the shouts died away as people waited in suspense to see the outcome of the final duel. There was nothing anyone could do but watch. It was deadly silent.

Will bounced up and down on the line to try and settle his nerves. He decided to dive this time, but he wasn't sure yet which way. As Pele loped towards him, he tried to pick up any little give-away sign about where the kicker would aim the ball. He didn't have a clue.

Whack!

The ball went to the right and Will dived – the opposite way. As he hit the ground, he heard the ball strike wood and the crowd erupted with noise.

Pele had hit the post!

The ball rebounded to Pele and he slammed it into the net, but he knew that it wouldn't count. There were no second chances. The damage was done.

The whole Colford first-team squad ran towards Will and danced madly about in the penalty area.

As Pele walked away in dismay, both Josh and Baz patted him on the shoulder. They realized it wasn't worth trying to speak to him at that moment. Baz, especially, could hardly guess how Pele must be feeling. He'd felt bad enough himself after his own miss. This must be ten times worse.

Chopper didn't care about Pele's feelings. 'You idiot!' he screamed at him. 'Now we've lost the Cup.'

The Lynton teacher overheard and was very angry. 'You've got no right to say anything like that. You refused to take one yourself, captain, so don't go blaming anybody else.'

Five minutes later, Josh stepped proudly forward to receive the trophy on behalf of his team and his school. He held it up high to cheers from the Colford supporters.

Even Mr Smith was smiling. 'Great stuff, lads,' he called out as they went up one by one to be awarded their medals. Then he quickly corrected himself, 'er … and Charlotte, of course too. Well played, all of you!'

'What a way to end the season!' whooped Michael, when they were back in the changing room.

'Not quite the end,' Josh grinned; 'we've still got that other little matter to sort out tomorrow, remember.'

Out of habit, they checked round to make sure the teacher hadn't heard them mention Sunday football. But for once, Mr Smith didn't mind. He was sitting on a bench nursing the trophy with a silly grin on his face. He seemed to have forgotten all about his shopping.

'Don't worry, I know how important that game is to you as well,' he said. 'I might even come and watch it myself.'

Michael gazed down happily at the silver medal in his hand and he gave it a squeeze. It was the first one that he had won in his short football career so far – but he was determined that there would be many more to come in the future.

'Starting tomorrow!' he promised himself, secretly.

6

Sunday sweeper

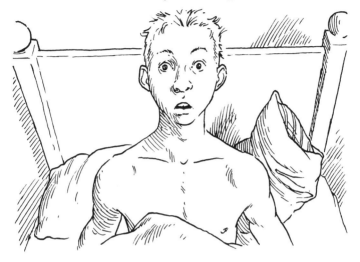

'Michael! Wake up, Michael!'

His mother's repeated call up the stairs finally gained his attention.

'Time to get up, sleepy-head. It's ten o'clock.'

Michael panicked and sat bolt upright in bed. He thought he must have overslept and missed the start of the Cup Final. Then he realized that it was Sunday and the Rangers match didn't kick off until the afternoon.

He breathed a huge sigh of relief and sank back into the pillow.

He tried to remember what he had been dreaming about – a mixture of the Final and the promotion battle with the Dynamos. His penalty in the shoot-out had been replayed several times in his sleep – and he'd scored every time.

Michael slid a hand underneath his pillow until it closed upon something small and hard – his winner's medal. He looked at it just to make sure it hadn't all been a dream. Then he smiled. It was real all right.

* * *

It was a telephone call a little while later that cast a shadow over the day ahead.

As Michael was eating a bowl of cereal, his dad came into the kitchen, grim-faced.

'What's the matter?' asked Michael.

'Just heard that Dinesh can't play. He took a knock in the Final and the injury has stiffened up overnight.'

Mr Medway helped to run Forest Rangers along with the father of Tom Butler, the Rangers' right full-back.

'I can't remember Dinesh getting hurt,' said Michael.

'No, nor can I. He must have felt OK at the time, or I'm sure he would have said something to us.'

'Dinesh played well yesterday – and he scored. We're going to miss him in midfield.'

His dad nodded. 'Better ring Mr Butler and decide what to do. It gives somebody else a chance, I suppose.'

'Adam?'

'Hmm … could be. He's done a good job as sub the last few games. He tackles well – gets stuck in. With you playing sweeper, Adam could cover behind you when you move forward to join an attack.'

'We might need some extra cover in defence with people like Baz and Pele coming at us.'

Michael was looking forward to playing against Baz.

The first time their Sunday sides met, Baz failed to get on the score-sheet. Michael knew that his friend was keen to make up for that; and Michael was just as keen to make sure he suffered another blank day.

His other memories of that game were not so good. Dynamos won it 3-1. Although Michael had scored Rangers' goal, he'd also headed one into his own net!

Rangers were now out for revenge in the return match on their home ground. The fixture list could hardly have worked out better. Everything was at stake. The top two teams in the division were playing each other in the final game of the season for the League Championship title.

Josh's Dynamos were just one point clear and already sure of promotion. But Michael's Rangers also had to look over their shoulders. The team in third place, Gosden Tigers, had a better goal difference and could ruin their chances of promotion, if Rangers were to lose.

Michael couldn't bear the thought of that happening. The Tigers were captained by Chopper!

When the phone rang again at midday, it was Josh.

'Hi there, Mike. How are you feeling?'

'Fine. A few bruises where Chopper left his mark, but fit and ready to thrash you this afternoon!'

'You've got to be joking! We'll win easily again. I heard Dinesh is out.'

'How do you know that?'

'I bumped into him this morning in the street.'

'Not on your bike, I hope!' Michael laughed. 'I bet that's really why he's injured.'

'Don't be stupid. I just saw him limping along and he told me the good news.'

'Don't you mean the bad news?'

'Not from our point of view,' Josh sniggered. 'He's one of your best players. I just rang to rub it in, but you've given me a great idea.'

'What's that?'

'I think I'll go for another ride round on my bike and see if I can find Will and run him over!'

Josh's laughter was still ringing in Michael's ears as he hung up. 'Huh! He won't find it very funny later when we take the title off them,' the Rangers captain muttered under his breath. 'It'll be our turn to laugh then.'

When Michael arrived at the recreation ground, the first person he saw there was Charlotte.

'I've come to cheer you on,' she grinned.

Michael was taken aback. 'Why not Josh and Baz's lot?'

'Well, there are more players from our school in your Rangers side than in the Dynamos. And they've got Pele and Liam and a couple of other Lynton lads. Makes sense.'

'Guess so, but we've got Hanif playing for us, you know.'

'I know. I quite like him. He's got a nice smile.'

'Now I see why you're really here, Charlie,' he teased her. 'I'll tell Hanif you fancy him!'

'Don't you dare. I'll start cheering for Dynamos if you go and do that.'

Baz was the first of the Dynamos to turn up. 'Hi, guys!' he called out. 'Who are you supporting, Charlie?'

She shot Michael a warning glance. 'Don't know yet. It all depends.'

'Depends who's winning, you mean,' Baz grinned.

'Pity you're not playing today, Charlie,' said Michael. 'It's a stupid rule not allowing mixed teams in the Sunday League. Works OK in primary school football.'

Baz agreed. 'We'd have signed Charlie up for Dynamos like a shot if we could.'

'Not if the Rangers had got to her first, you wouldn't.'

'Oh! Nice to have you boys fighting over me,' she giggled, 'but I'm going to find myself an all-girls team to play for on Sundays next season.'

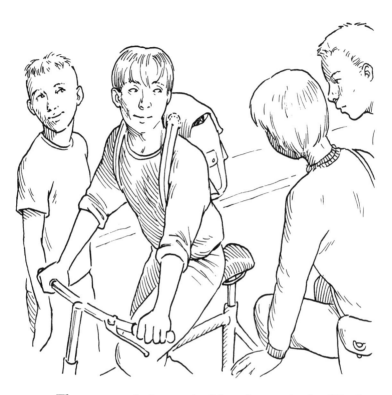

They were interrupted by the arrival of Josh on his bike. He skidded to a halt beside them.

'Hope Will managed to escape you,' Michael greeted him.

'Only just!' Josh laughed. 'Great win yesterday, eh? It'll be hard for this game to live up to it.'

'At least it can't go to penalties,' said Baz. 'I couldn't stand going through all that again.'

'Yeah, I hope Pele's got over his miss by now,' said Josh. 'Anyway, victory this afternoon will help to cheer him up.'

'Don't count your chickens,' put in Michael. 'We want to win the title as much as you lot do.'

'Yeah, but you've got Chopper's Tigers hot on your tail. If they win their match, you've got to get at least a point to stay ahead of them. You'll be happy with a draw today, I bet.'

'So would we,' Baz admitted. 'That'd make us champions.'

'I want to finish in style with a big win.'

'Even if that might stop Mike's team getting promoted?' asked Charlie.

'That'd make it even better!' Josh said with a broad grin. 'Sorry, but friendship doesn't come into it. Mike wouldn't expect any favours from us and we won't from him.'

'That's the way it should be,' Michael agreed. 'We don't want anybody like Chopper accusing us of fixing the result. We're going all out for a win too.'

'Is that why you're playing in defence?' asked Josh, cheekily. 'Sounds more like trying to avoid defeat!'

'Don't worry, you'll be seeing plenty of me up in attack as well,' Michael said. 'Best of both worlds, I reckon, playing as sweeper. It means I'm always in the thick of the action at both ends of the pitch.'

The joking continued between them as they strolled towards the changing hut. On a table outside the hut was the gleaming championship shield.

'Wonder which one of us will be lifting that up after the match?' said Josh.

'You had all the glory yesterday with the cup,' Michael replied. 'Don't be greedy.'

'I was just practising. I want to do it again today.'

Michael pulled a face. 'We'll see about that.'

The boys split up to go towards their separate changing rooms. Josh paused and gazed out over the pitch where they had enjoyed hundreds of kickabouts over the years.

'This is where the joking stops, Mike,' he said. 'It's the big showdown now. May the best team win, eh?'

His rival captain nodded. 'Right – so long as that's the Rangers!'

7
Kick-off

'C'mon, the Greens!'

'Up the Reds!'

The two teams were given a noisy welcome by their parents and friends as they came out of the changing hut at the same time. In contrast to the plain all-green outfit of Forest Rangers, the Dynamos' kit had a large red star on the front of their shirts.

As the players warmed up, Baz pointed out a familiar figure on the touchline. 'Old Smithy is here, look, like he said he would be.'

'I just hope he doesn't start yelling stupid remarks,' said Josh. 'Y'know, the way he normally does.'

'No, he can leave that sort of thing to our parents today,' Baz said with a grin.

Dinesh was there too. He wandered among his team-mates as they stretched their muscles and passed a few footballs around. He tried to join in but his ankle was too sore.

'How did it happen?' asked Tom Butler, who went to a different school in the town.

'I reckon it was when Chopper kicked me in extra time.'

'Chopper? Ah, right, I know who you mean. That great big kid who fouls anybody who goes near him – captain of Gosden Tigers as well.'

'That's the one. Remember when we played the Tigers here? He nearly got sent off for kicking Mike into touch.'

'I remember. I kept well out of his way after that.'

'Wish I'd done that yesterday,' sighed Dinesh, rubbing his ankle. 'It's thanks to him that Adam's playing now instead of me.'

'Chopper's a nut case,' Hanif added, overhearing what they were saying, 'and a bully. He's always throwing his weight about at school.'

'So why do you put up with him?'

Hanif shrugged. 'What can you do? If you say anything, he gets his gang on to you. Nobody else from Lynton will play for Tigers because he's with them.'

'It's up to us to make sure he has a bad weekend then,' said Tom, 'missing promotion on top of losing the Cup Final.'

'I'll have to make sure I stay out of his way myself if that happens,' Hanif grinned.

Michael and Josh briefly shook hands before the toss. 'Good luck,' said Michael.

'And you.'

Neither of them meant it. Their friendship had to be put on hold for the next hour.

Rangers kicked off with a slight breeze in their favour, but conditions were perfect for a game of football. They won a corner from their first attack and Michael trotted upfield to add his extra height in the penalty area.

He timed his jump well to beat Josh at the far post and head the ball towards goal. Liam was alert to the danger and tipped it over the bar for another corner.

'Well, we've made a promising start,' said Mr Medway to his co-manager. 'Let's hope the lads can keep it up.'

Tom's father nodded. 'Aye, it should be a good battle between your Mike and that Josh.'

Josh won round two of their contest. He met the corner first this time and headed the ball firmly away.

'Bye, bye, Mike,' he called out, 'off you go. Get back in defence. See you.'

'You sure will. I'll be back.'

It was at least ten minutes, however, before Michael enjoyed the luxury of crossing the halfway line again. And by that time, Dynamos was one goal up.

Rangers' attacks became rare as the visitors kept them pinned in their own half of the pitch. Liam could have brought a book out to read during this spell of almost constant pressure on the Rangers goal. Will would not even have had time to glance at the title.

The busy Rangers' keeper had made a number of excellent saves. The best of these was from a shot by Pele which was deflected off Adam's knee. Will was wrong-footed at first, but somehow managed to twist round and stop the ball right on the line.

The shot that beat him was a beauty. Tom had the thankless job of marking Pele and the star winger was giving him a terrible time.

Pele set up the goal by slipping the ball through Tom's legs and then dragging Michael out of position. As the sweeper moved across to try and cut him off, Pele skilfully switched the ball into the gap that he had left in the middle.

The pass was so good that Baz didn't even need to touch the ball before he shot. Will had left his line, but he had no chance of reaching Baz's first-time strike that zipped low into the corner of the net.

'Yeesss!' Baz screamed in delight, a clenched fist raised to the sky. His pleasure in scoring was even greater with it being against so many of his school-mates.

Dynamos seemed to relax slightly after
that first goal. They sat back on their lead for
a while and this allowed the home team to
recover. Michael pushed further forward,
striding out of defence with the ball to start
up their own attacks. He also had a long-
range effort at goal himself that Liam was
glad to see fly just wide of the target.

Josh was keeping a very tight rein on Hanif. Every time the striker tried to find space to receive a pass, Josh seemed stuck to him like a shadow that he couldn't shake off. Even when Hanif did succeed in getting the ball, he wasn't allowed to have it for long.

'Great tackle, Josh!' came a shout from the touchline, after the centre-back had won the ball off Hanif again. It was only after he had made the clearance that Josh realized the praise was from Mr Smith. The captain could hardly believe it!

With Hanif so quiet, the Rangers' attack was as blunt as a pencil stub. The Dynamos got back on top and Michael was kept busy in defence once more. He swept up all the loose bits and pieces that other defenders missed, but a few minutes before half-time Pele broke free and went bombing for goal.

The winger's pace left poor Tom for dead and not even Michael or Adam could catch him. The next thing Rangers knew, the ball was spinning in the bottom of their net.

Will had barely moved, the shot was hit with such power.

Pele wheeled crazily away towards the corner flag as usual, screaming at full volume. 'GOOAALL! GOOAALL!'

The Rangers stared at each other in horror. Pele's wild delight seemed to signal the end of their promotion hopes.

'C'mon, Greens, we can't afford to lose this game,' cried their captain. 'We've got to grab some goals of our own.'

The situation for Rangers at half-time was desperate. They were 2-0 down and the news from elsewhere did nothing to raise their spirits. A spy at the Tigers' match rang up Mr Butler on his mobile phone to report that their nearest rivals were leading by the same score.

'Looks like we're in a spot of bother, lads,' said Mr Butler, stating the obvious. 'We'll have to change our tactics now and take some risks in the second half.'

Mr Medway agreed. 'You know what the old saying is in football – attack is the best form of defence!'

8

Go for goals

'Rangers! Rangers! Rangers!'

Charlie and Dinesh led the chants to spur on the home team as the second half was about to get under way.

'Sounds like our fans have woken up at last,' said Hanif. 'We're going to need their support to get us back into this game.'

Michael grinned. 'You've got your own fan club over there.'

'What do you mean?'

'See that girl in the blue tracksuit jumping up and down?'

Hanif peered across towards Charlie. 'I think I've seen her somewhere before.'

'You have. Last time you saw Charlie, she was wearing a blue football kit. She's the one who scored our equalizer yesterday.'

Hanif shrugged. 'OK – so what?'

'She's come here just to watch you play. Only don't tell her I said so – she'd kill me!'

Hanif didn't reply. The whistle went for the kick-off and he tapped the ball forward to his new strike partner.

Josh was quick to spot the double threat to the Dynamos.

'Looks like they mean business this half,' he muttered to himself. 'Mike's playing striker again.'

The Rangers had made many changes to boost their chances of scoring. They'd been forced to switch from a sweeper system to a bold 3-2-5 formation. Michael was leading their five-man attack, with Tom also pushed up on to the right wing.

They were going all out for goals.

The gamble nearly came unstuck straight away. There were large holes now in their own defence and Pele suddenly popped up in one of them. He could hardly believe how much extra space he had in front of goal when Baz gave him the ball.

Perhaps Pele had too much time to think. He delayed his shot just a fraction too long and Adam was able to put in a challenge. It was enough to knock the winger off-balance and the ball crashed against the post. Will gratefully hugged the rebound to his chest.

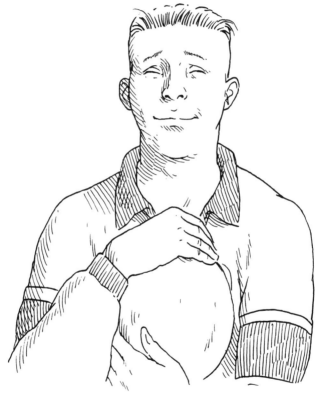

'Phew! That was close,' gasped Mr Medway. 'A few centimetres the other way and that might have been curtains for us.'

'We're going to need a bit of good fortune,' said Mr Butler, 'so let's just hope that it's our lucky day.'

It certainly seemed to be his son's. Tom was very glad to leave the task of marking Pele to Adam, and run loose on the wing himself for a change. In the Rangers' first two attacks, the ball didn't come his way, but when it did in the next, he wasn't quite sure what to do with it.

If Tom was confused, the Dynamos' full-back had no idea what the new winger was going to attempt. They both hesitated to make the first move and it gave Tom time to look up and see who was nearby for a pass.

He was on his own. Everybody else seemed to be heading for the penalty area.

Tom panicked. He didn't have the confidence to try and dribble past the defender, so he leaned back and booted the ball hard and high – too hard, too high. It sailed beyond all his team-mates and appeared to be going out of play.

The groans from the Rangers supporters suddenly turned to cheers. The ball swirled and dipped at the last moment and dropped over Liam's hands into the net. It was Tom's first goal of the season!

He wasn't the only one rooted to the spot in shock. It took the others several seconds to realize what had happened as well. He was then buried beneath a ton of bodies.

'Wow!' he gasped, half-suffocated, when he struggled free, 'now I know what it feels like to score – squashed!'

The goal changed the mood of the game. Now that the Rangers had scented blood, they were hungry for more. They enjoyed their best spell of the game and stretched Josh's well-organized defence to the limit.

'C'mon, we still need another goal at least,' Michael urged his team. 'One's not enough, we've got to equalize!'

The captain hadn't given up hope of winning the title. He felt they might yet score a couple more and snatch a win, but deep down, he would settle for a draw now. A single point was all they needed to earn promotion.

A third goal for the Dynamos, however, would kill off their dreams. And Baz almost became their assassin.

Rangers were caught on the break by a swift raid and Baz beat three players on a superb solo dribble. Only Will's full-length dive prevented the goal.

His fingertips just turned the ball around his left-hand post.

Josh went up for the corner in the hope of clinching his team's victory. Michael followed him; dogging his footsteps like a faithful hound. Josh darted about in the area to try and lose his marker, but he couldn't wriggle free. Michael stayed as close to him as the star on his shirt.

As Baz's corner came over, they both made contact with the ball at the same time. It squirted away and dropped to the feet of Pele, the last person that Rangers should have left unmarked.

Pele hit the ball on the half-volley and it screamed low towards goal through a forest of legs. Will never even saw it coming.

'GOOAA...!' Pele's war-cry died in his throat.

Adam had scrambled the ball off the line. He stuck out a foot to block the shot and then hacked it clear of danger.

'Thanks, Adam,' cried Will, 'you saved us there.'

News came through on the phone that the Tigers had won their match 4-1, but the managers kept it to themselves. The players didn't need any extra motivation.

'They know what they have to do,' said Mr Butler. 'It's up to them.'

Michael was doing his best to remain calm, but it wasn't easy at a time like this.

After their narrow escape, the captain made the decision to return to the role of sweeper to bolster the defence.

'We just can't afford to let another goal in now,' he murmured. 'Every time Dynamos attack, they look as if they're going to score.'

He also felt he wasn't seeing enough of the ball himself in attack. He was being too tightly marked, either by Josh or the other defenders. Whenever he managed to get past one of them, he ran straight into another. As sweeper, he had more space to carry the ball forward into midfield, and then join in the attack from a deeper position.

His father glanced nervously at his watch. 'Only a few minutes left, plus any stoppage time the ref adds on,' he said to people around him. 'We're leaving it very late.'

Michael realized how late it must be when he saw the referee check his watch too. Baz was on the ball, dribbling around and using up precious seconds until Michael stepped in and whipped the ball off his toes.

He advanced over the halfway line with it, then switched play out to Tom on the right.

Tom moved the ball on to Hanif who had his back to goal with Josh snapping at his heels. The striker shielded it skilfully as Michael came steaming up in support, demanding the ball.

Hanif released it into his path and the sweeper took it in his stride.

'Close him down!' cried Josh in vain.

If there had been a police camera trap on the pitch, Michael might have been stopped for speeding. He burst past the final defender and found himself one-on-one with the goalkeeper. And this time his boot stayed on.

Michael flicked the ball past the keeper as Liam dived down at his feet. He almost tripped as Liam's arm caught him, but somehow he kept his balance and regained control of the ball. The empty goal yawned in front of him and he struck from a metre out. The net bulged! It was the most wonderful feeling in the world.

His team-mates swarmed around him, but Michael waved them away. He also told Tom to return to his full-back position.

'Concentrate, men,' he ordered, 'don't let this slip now. It's not over yet.'

The final two minutes were as nervous as any in the whole season – for both teams. Each would have loved to score the winner, but neither could risk making a silly mistake that would cost them the game. Defences had to be kept tight.

At last the referee ended everybody's jitters with a shrill blast on the whistle. Supporters ran on to the pitch to congratulate the players and celebrate the 2-2 score-line.

They were all happy. A point apiece made Dynamos champions and also gave promotion to Rangers as runners-up.

And Charlie had a good excuse to go up to shy Hanif and give him a special hug of delight! Michael and Josh wrapped their arms around each other too. They could be friends again now.

'Fantastic!' Josh yelled at the top of his voice. 'Nobody deserved to lose a great game like that. What a match!'

'What a weekend!' Michael shouted back, just as carried away by all the excitement. 'I can't wait till next season!'

About the author

The best part of my job as
a teacher was all the sports
coaching I used to do. I
still miss that, but make
up for it now by writing
lots of football books for
soccer-mad readers.

I hope you've found
this story exciting. It
might even have made you want to go out
and practise your own ball skills too.

And I'm not just talking to the boys here.
Football's a great game for girls too. Enjoy
your reading, everybody – and your playing!